FAIR DINKUM!

INTRODUCTION AND COMMENTARY BY

H.G. NELSON

AUSSIE
SLANG

FAIR
DINKUM!

CELEBRATING

NATIONAL LIBRARY
OF AUSTRALIA
PUBLISHING

50 YEARS

Published by NLA Publishing
Canberra   ACT   2600

ISBN: 9781922507556

The National Library of Australia acknowledges Australia's First Nations Peoples—the First Australians—as the Traditional Owners and Custodians of this land and gives respect to the Elders—past and present—and through them to all Australian Aboriginal and Torres Strait Islander people.

Commissioning publisher: Susan Hall
Editor: Amelia Hartney
Designer: Louise Dews, Mike Ellott
Image coordinator: Jemma Posch
Printed in China through Asia Pacific Offset

Find out more about NLA Publishing at nla.gov.au/national-library-publishing.

A catalogue record for this book is available from the National Library of Australia

G'DAY!

Language is a powerful weapon and its explosive propellant is slang. As this excellent collection of slang words and phrases demonstrates, Australians have left a unique yellow and green mark on the rich history of the English language.

Our top-of-the-table position at international forums has been all the more notable for our outstanding linguistic contributions: 'Look out world,' we bellowed in late 2014, 'Team Australia is on the burst coming through with a shirtfront!' This demonstrated that the lucky country can still punch above its weight when push comes to shove on the world's linguistic stage.

Unfortunately, time rolls on. Juicy dollops of slang eventually lose their grunt and poke, drop off the twig of time and are consigned to the ashtray of history. While most good slang is welded to the tempo of the times, the language of our grandparents can still get us misty-eyed (even if some of it has all the menace of limp iceberg lettuce and is as cryptic as the poetry of Catullus).

'TEAM AUSTRALIA'

'HOOF ON THE TILL'

I'm not sure when I first understood the dry powder power of slang. I probably got thumped once or twice in the school playground on the way up, but I always thought I'd held my own in a stink if I could get a jab in with the tongue— before taking one and going down for the count.

Years later on the radio, as I waddled along the sporting beat, slang was a key to the insider's view of every competition. Sports buffs may not have a clue about what's happening on the park but well-chosen slang allows even the novices to appear plugged into the source. The colourful use of slang can have the audience leaning forward wondering, 'Did they really just say that? What on earth did they mean?'

For most of my working life, I've been lucky enough to work in the sporting coverage of radio and television. Shows like *This Sporting Life* (Triple J), *The Dream* (Channel Seven) and *Festival of the Boot* (Triple J and ABC NewsRadio) allowed my colleague, Rampaging Roy Slaven, and me to roam across the dial bending the language and creating our own slang. With several hours of airtime every week, it was possible to muscle new meanings onto simple words and phrases, allowing us to reset the linguistic landscape. There are rich pickings for language freaks in a world where too much sport is barely enough.

Understanding sporting slang makes you a member of the crew. This slang is crammed with a grim humour—Australians love to laugh at adversity. It's impossible to imagine the glorious uncertainty of horseracing without its dense and specific slang. Those on the losing end of the punt can be philosophical about having the shirt ripped from their back with the aid of it. Rich racing slang is a common language that's easy enough to rapidly unravel—take concepts like 'hoof on the till', 'be on me next time', 'smoking the pipe', 'smelling the field' and that fabulous image of a four-legged conveyance 'growing an extra leg in the wet'.

Rugby league coverage drips with slang. 'Going the grope', 'applying the squirrel grip' and 'reaching for the Christmas handshake' all refer to rugby league moves where the wedding tackle is the focus of the attack. This is considered very poor form, as the night tools are very important when the tune turns to horizontal folk dancing post hooter. After a vigorous Christmas handshake or a dismal performance, players are advised to 'go into the Room of Mirrors' and have 'a good hard look at themselves'. If a bustling ball-playing prop is tackled head high around 'the bonce', concussion often results, requiring a trip to 'the half dream room'. Once inside, coaches always stress the importance of being able to find 'the doorknob' that allows the mind to escape back to what is understood in rugby league circles as 'normality'.

'SQUIRREL GRIP'

'HULLO BOYS'

In 2000, I found myself in the odd position of being able to contribute a whole raft of slang to the world of words during the Sydney Olympics when covering the gymnastics competition. Terms like 'battered sav', 'hullo boys', 'crazy date', 'Dutch wink', 'spinning date', 'flat bag' and 'honey I'm home' were all moves tagged by Roy and me when fit young mat stars from all over the world went for gold. It took the viewers very little time to pick up the language we layered onto a sport that was tricky for the average punter to understand.

Slang does not always take off. Roy and I over the years have tried to popularise 'sloop pointing north', which ideally occurs during post-hooter horizontal folk dancing. We have failed. The boudoir is a very crowded linguistic market place in which we sadly could make little headway.

Slang has a great regional component. Because of the nation's size, South Australian slang is different from that of New South Wales, Western Australia's is vastly different from Victoria's, and so on. Different sports, different foods, different beer, different ambitions and different working circumstances all generate their own local linguistic responses. 'The Doctor' is a breeze that cools Perth on hot summer days.

'The coathanger' refers to the Sydney Harbour Bridge. Adelaide has 'fritz', a local luncheon meat, and 'the Kitchener bun'—two locally made linguistic gap fillers that baffle visitors, but have sustained generations of South Australian school kids. Melbourne has the 'G' where they play 'the Grannie' on that 'one day in September'. And so it goes.

In the modern social media world, state-based differences are being broken down rapidly. Everything and everyone is as close as the mobile phone in the hip pocket or handbag. But let's hope they don't all disappear as the slanguage of the future will be poorer without lively, local contributions.

Finally, an example of how quickly the whole caper moves on: the term, 'a Bradbury', indicating that an event was won because only one competitor was left standing at the finish line, was popularised after Steven Bradbury's amazing speed skating win in the 2002 Winter Olympics. Today, the term needs a lot of explanation.

H.G. NELSON

LEARN MORE

Readers can learn more Australian slang, and find out about the etymology of slang words and phrases, using the following excellent online resources:

Macquarie Dictionary,
www.macquariedictionary.com.au

'Meanings and Origins of Australian Words and Idioms',
Australian National Dictionary Centre,
Australian National University,
slll.cass.anu.edu.au/centres/andc/meanings-origins

FAIR DINKUM

truthful; fair; possessing Australian honesty; are you telling me the truth?

Dinkum was British Midlands dialect for 'work' and 'fair dinkum' is probably derived from the idea of 'a fair day's dinkum'.

HAPPY LITTLE VEGEMITES

*happy Australians,
usually children*

**H.G.'s
SPRAY**

The Australian spreadable
yeast extract market has several
competitors. There's the English
Marmite and the Australian
so-sweet-it-may-as-well-be-American
Promite. Both these blow-ins are
overrated rubbish. It's completely
un-Australian to be seen spreading
these inferior products onto
Mallee-grown wholegrain toast.

From an advertising
jingle for Vegemite,
Happy Little Vegemites,
first aired in 1954.

CHEEKY LITTLE POSSUM

an incorrigible but humorous and endearing person, usually a child

YEAH, NAH

*yes, I understand,
but no*

AS USEFUL
AS LIPS ON
A CHICKEN

useless

CROOK AS A CHOOK

very sick

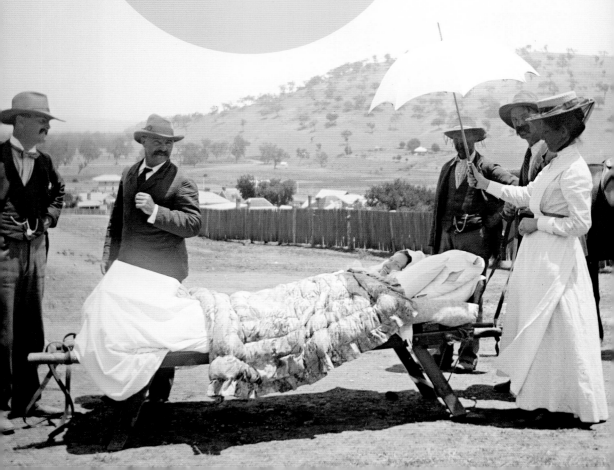

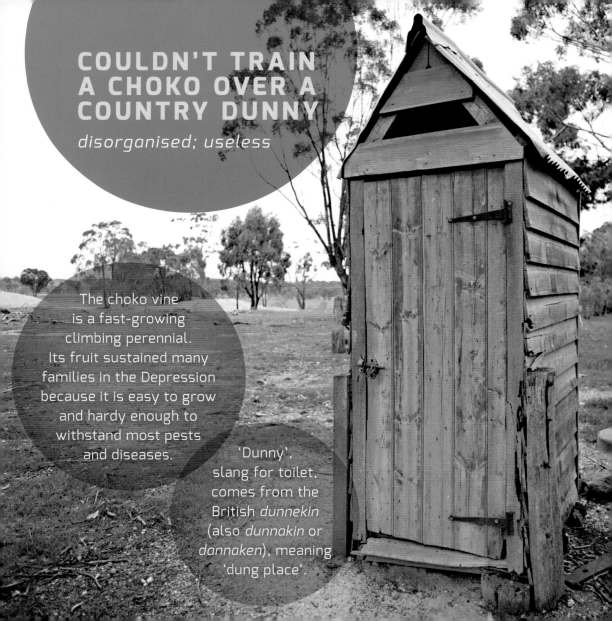

COULDN'T TRAIN A CHOKO OVER A COUNTRY DUNNY

disorganised; useless

The choko vine is a fast-growing climbing perennial. Its fruit sustained many families in the Depression because it is easy to grow and hardy enough to withstand most pests and diseases.

'Dunny', slang for toilet, comes from the British *dunnekin* (also *dunnakin* or *dannaken*), meaning 'dung place'.

**I HOPE YOUR CHOOKS
TURN INTO EMUS
AND KICK YOUR
DUNNY DOWN**

I wish you bad luck

A FEW SANDWICHES SHORT OF A PICNIC

stupid

COULDN'T ORGANISE A CHOOK RAFFLE AT A POULTRY FARM

disorganised; useless

MAD AS A CUT SNAKE

insane; very angry

MAKE A PROPER GALAH OF YOURSELF

make a fool of yourself

HE'S GOT A KANGAROO LOOSE IN THE TOP PADDOCK

crazy; stupid

GO TROPPO

go mad

Originating in the Second World War to describe the effect of prolonged engagements in the tropical jungles of South-East Asia on Australian servicemen.

AS SLOW AS A WET WEEK

very slow;
boring

Given that the nation's in perpetual drought, this snap carries a boot load of irony. In a week that drags on forever, sometimes the most interesting thing to happen is the numbers spinning 'round on the petrol bowser.

H.G.'s SPRAY

Cooee was a locating cry in Dharug, the Aboriginal language in the Sydney area.

HIKERS TRACKS

TO LONG POINT ½ M.
TO RIVER 2½ M.

WITHIN COOEE

*not too far away
(distance, goal)*

BOPEECHEE

ALICE SPRINGS 497 M.
312 M. PORT PIRIE

WOOP
WOOP

*a very
remote place*

BACK OF BOURKE

a very remote place

H.G.'s SPRAY

There are remote patches of dirt across this sun-drenched land. But the nation's shrinking. Planes can go everywhere and motorbikes plug the gaps. Digital communication makes Bourke seem just over the horizon instead of in the middle of nowhere. Although Oodnadatta still requires two hands to find on the map.

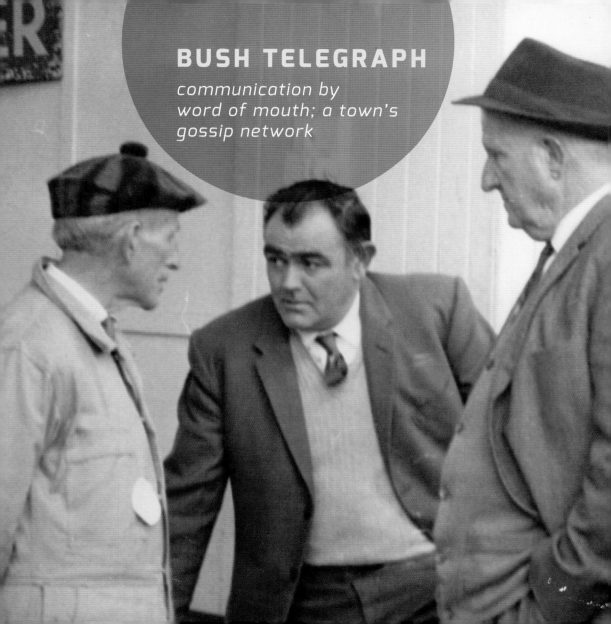

BUSH TELEGRAPH

*communication by
word of mouth; a town's
gossip network*

SEE YOU ROUND LIKE A RISSOLE

*goodbye;
see you later*

CARK IT

break down; die

CLAPPED OUT OLD BOMB

an old car in poor working order; a broken-down car

**CHUCK
A U-EY**

make a U-turn

Bush Week was a festival first held in Sydney in 1920, during which large numbers of people from the country would visit. The original meaning of this phrase (do you think I'm stupid?) implies that the visitors weren't always treated fairly by their city counterparts.

GIVE IT
A CRACK
try

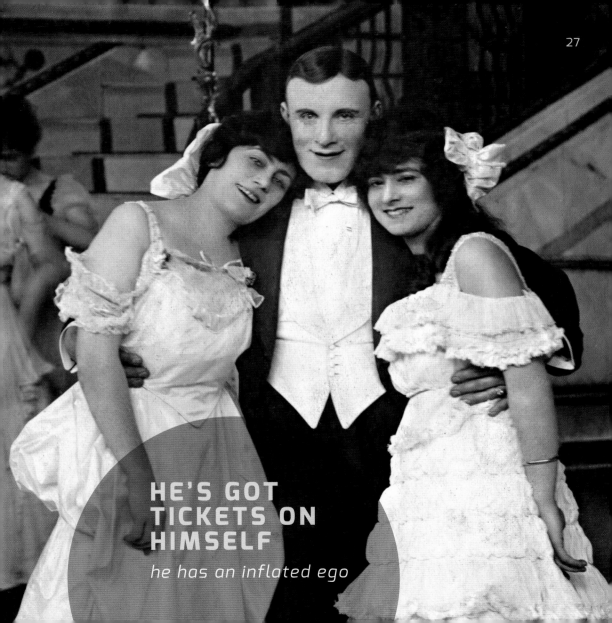

HE'S GOT TICKETS ON HIMSELF

he has an inflated ego

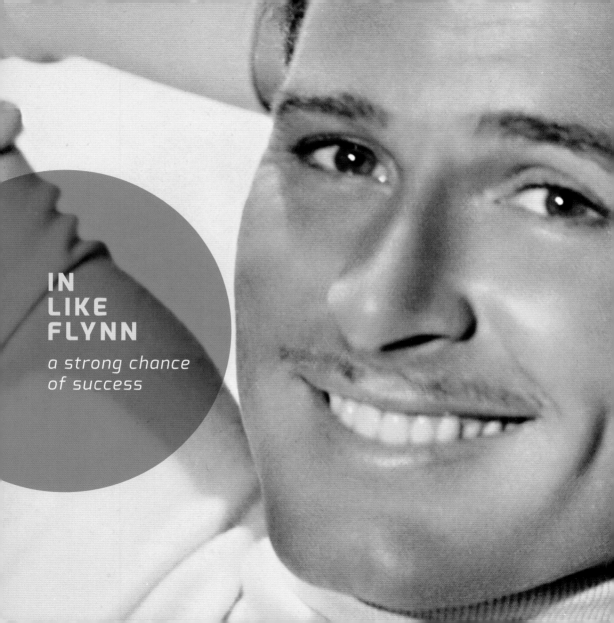

IN
LIKE
FLYNN

*a strong chance
of success*

Errol Flynn (1909–1959) was an Australian actor who shot to stardom in Hollywood playing romantic swashbuckling roles.

This phrase is thought to have emerged in the Second World War, perhaps as a humorous nod to Flynn's reputation as a ladies' man.

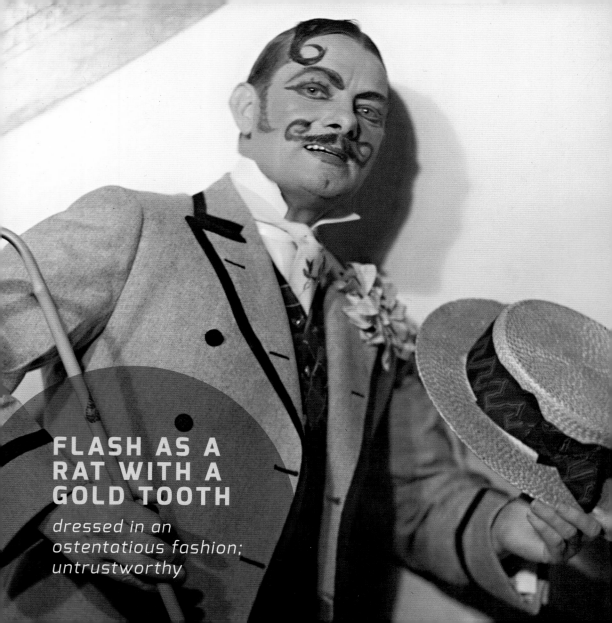

FLASH AS A RAT WITH A GOLD TOOTH

dressed in an ostentatious fashion; untrustworthy

PASH

*a passionate
kiss*

TRUE
BLUE

authentically
Australian

No one went as far or as long as
Slim Dusty. He made Australia his
backyard. His classic, *A Pub with No Beer*,
was once considered a starter for the
national anthem. In the twenty-first
century, when the world wants to be
just like us, it's a crime not to be able
to recite the first three verses of
this rural hospitality epic.

G'DAY
hello

SUSS
*suspicious;
suspect*

GRILLED CHOPS

STEAK AND EGGS

T SALAD
CE CREAM

FISH AND CHIPS

SAUSAGES AND MASHED POTATO

TUCKER

food

Used since the 1850s to refer to something that can be tucked away in your stomach.

SANGER

sandwich

ALL FROTH, NO BEER

superficial

FAIR GO

be fair; a fair opportunity

FAIR SHAKE OF THE SAUCE BOTTLE

be fair

SNAG
sausage

DRINKING WITH THE FLIES
drinking alone

BARBECUE STOPPER

an unexpected or
shocking piece of
information

LIKE FLIES ROUND A DUNNY DOOR

*a throng of people
attracted to something*

WRAP YOUR LAUGHING GEAR ROUND THAT

eat that

FULL AS A GOOG

*sated with
food or alcohol*

**H.G.'s
SPRAY**

These two lads, Cyril and Cedric,
have done a lot of work with
the fork and the twenty-ounce
glass. They've been at it for years.
To construct this style of cantilevered
verandah over the tool shed takes
years of effort including the design
phase, getting council permission
and then all the heavy lifting.
But the results are world class.

Possibly connected
to the Scottish
children's word, *goggie*,
meaning 'egg'.

**A MAN'S
NOT A
CAMEL**

I need a drink

GET A GONG

win an award

Derived from *vin blanc*,
meaning 'white wine' in French,
pronounced as 'van blonk'
and then shortened to 'plonk'
by Australian soldiers
in the First World War.

PLONK

wine;
cheap wine

**FLAT OUT
LIKE A LIZARD
DRINKING**

*very busy;
exhausted*

LOWER THAN A SNAKE'S BELLY

despicable;
untrustworthy

MAD AS A GUMTREE FULL OF GALAHS

crazy

MOPEY AS A WET HEN

dispirited; glum

CROOKED AS A DOG'S HIND LEG

very dishonest

BALD AS A BANDICOOT

completely bald

LIKE A POSSUM UP A GUMTREE

*safe and content;
very quickly
(of movement)*

MISERABLE AS A SHAG ON A ROCK

very miserable

ON THE WALLABY

*on the move,
looking for work*

In 1860s Australia, men would
travel on foot across the
country seeking work, as if
following a wallaby's tracks.

LIKE A STUNNED MULLET

shocked: surprised

STONE THE CROWS!

wow!; I can't believe it!; I'm unimpressed

STREWTH!

that's shocking!;
wow!;
that was close!

H.G.'s SPRAY

Yesterday's acceptable swear word, overtaken, today, by 'Oh my God'. But bravely kept alive in the lingo of Alf from *Home and Away*, who appears to have a contract that requires him to blurt it once in every episode.

An abbreviated form of 'God's truth', originating in Britain.

COP A LOAD OF THAT!

look at that!

IT'S SO WINDY IT COULD BLOW A DOG OFF A CHAIN

it's very windy

H.G.'s
SPRAY

With climate on the move, this graphic expression is one that may get a second wind and become hip again. But our relationship with the four-legged community has changed so much that not many Spots are chained up these days. It's so windy it could blow Buster out of his day spa?

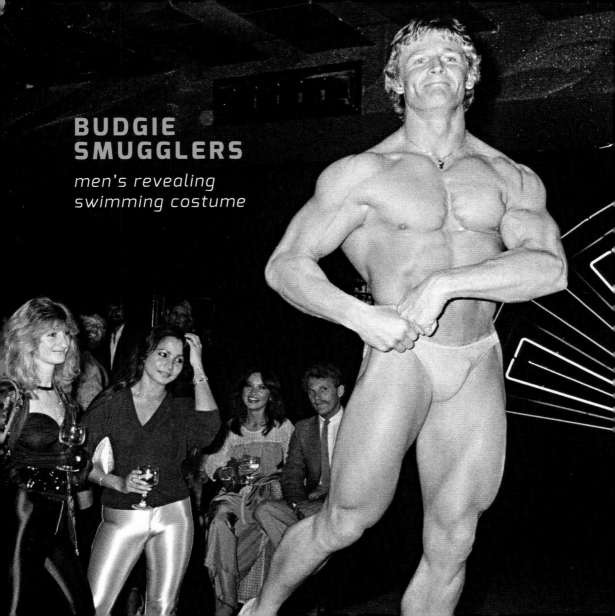

BUDGIE SMUGGLERS

*men's revealing
swimming costume*

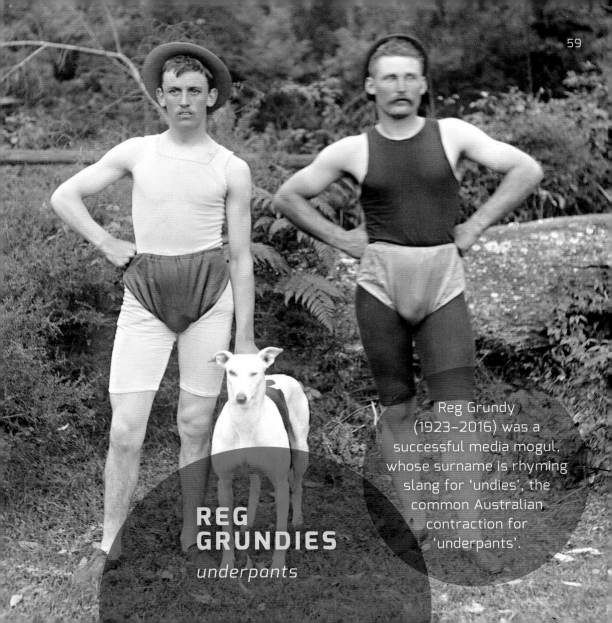

REG GRUNDIES

underpants

Reg Grundy (1923–2016) was a successful media mogul, whose surname is rhyming slang for 'undies', the common Australian contraction for 'underpants'.

DAG

*an unfashionable
but lovable
person*

A bludgeoner was a person who used a bludgeon as a weapon. This evolved to mean 'a prostitute's pimp', one living off the earnings of another.

BLUDGER

a person who doesn't contribute his or her fair share

BOGAN
*an uncultured
person lacking
class; a boor*

WOWSER

a person who is easily morally outraged; a prude; a killjoy

Possibly related to the British verb *wow*, meaning 'to complain' or perhaps an acronym standing for We Only Want Social Evils Righted. John Norton, editor of *Truth* magazine, claimed to have coined it in 1899.

DRONGO

an idiot

Probably after an Australian horse of the same name, which ran 37 races in the early 1920s without a win.

PANIC MERCHANT

a person who panics easily

DINKY-DI

*authentically
Australian*

DROPKICK

an idiot

BOOFHEAD

an idiot

SILLY DUFFER

*a person who has
made a silly mistake*

This phrase possibly evolved
from the Scottish *duffar*,
meaning 'a stupid person'.

OCKER

*stereotypically
unsophisticated
Australian*

I WOULDN'T BE DEAD FOR QUIDS

I'm enjoying life!

GOING OFF LIKE A FROG IN A SOCK

very successful (of an event);
losing your temper;
doing something very
energetically

RUNNING AROUND LIKE A CHOOK WITH ITS HEAD CUT OFF

panicking; overreacting

**FLAT
CHAT**
at full speed

OFF LIKE A BUCKET OF PRAWNS IN THE SUN

to leave quickly or soon

H.G.'s SPRAY

Mercifully refrigeration has been invented so this stylish slang response to any stink has gone the way of the Muttaburrasaurus. Of course one of the great Australian stories is the tale of keeping things cool. The Coolgardie safe and the Esky were great early attempts, but the Kelvinator brought it home. Not sure anyone could find buckets of prawns to go off in the sun round Nowra in this day and age.

CHUCK A WOBBLY

throw a tantrum;
lose your temper

HE COULD TALK UNDER WET CEMENT

he's extremely talkative

NOT ENOUGH
BRAINS TO
GIVE HIMSELF
A HEADACHE

stupid

BUGGER THAT FOR A JOKE

I can't accept that!

HAVE A WHINGE

complain

BETTER THAN A POKE IN THE EYE WITH A BURNT STICK

it's not that bad

NO WORRIES

that's okay; I don't mind

YOU'VE GOT BUCKLEY'S

you've got no chance of success

William Buckley (1780–1856) was an English convict who escaped and lived with the Wathaurung people of south-western Victoria for 32 years. Buckley's survival, thanks largely to the Indigenous peoples of the Bellarine Peninsula, was an improbable one. He eventually returned to European society.

THINGS ARE CROOK IN TALLAROOK

things are not going well

CHUCK A SICKIE

*take a day off
work as sick leave
even if not sick*

DON'T COME THE RAW PRAWN WITH ME!

*don't cheat or
lie to me*

FURPHY

*misleading or false, but
commonly believed, story*

During the First World War,
John Furphy's water carts were
the 'water coolers' of the day—
places where people would
congregate and gossip.

HARD YAKKA

hard work, usually physical labour

Originally a Yagara word, from the Brisbane region, but used in Australian English since the 1880s.

HE'S HAVING A BARRY CROCKER

things are not going well for him

Barry Crocker (b.1935) is an entertainer, whose surname is rhyming slang for 'shocker'.

GAME AS NED

*very brave
(also, foolishly so)*

Ned is one of this nation's greatest inventors. He was the man who cut a hole in the front of a rubbish bin and put it on his head when he saw the cops coming. 'Such is life' was one of his. It's a hell of a phrase to go out on.

H.G.'s
SPRAY

Edward 'Ned' Kelly (1854–1880) was an Australian bushranger who committed daring and brazen crimes across Victoria, before being caught, convicted and hanged at Old Melbourne Gaol.

SHE'LL BE RIGHT

things will be okay

SHE'S APPLES

everything's fine

Derived from the rhyming slang phrase for nice, 'apple and spice'.

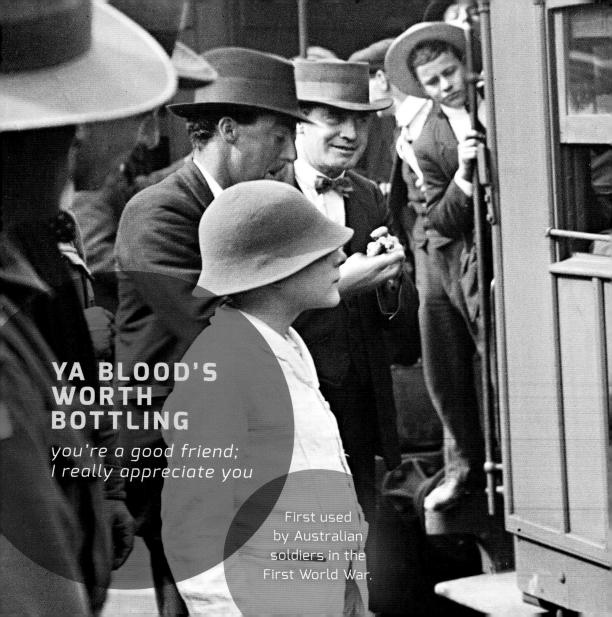

YA BLOOD'S
WORTH
BOTTLING

*you're a good friend;
I really appreciate you*

First used
by Australian
soldiers in the
First World War.

FACE LIKE A DROPPED PIE

very ugly

ROUGH
AS GUTS

coarse; uncouth

HEAD LIKE A BEATEN FAVOURITE

very ugly

H.G.'s SPRAY

Appearances have always been a rich source of slang. 'Face like a Mallee root' and 'face like a dropped pie' plus this gem remind us how creative the slang generated by our looks can be. Stating the bruised and bleeding obvious, the art of the sweet science is not to get punched continuously in the head, the process that results in a 'head like a beaten favourite'.

Originally from the Hindi *chāp*, meaning 'a stamp or brand', the phrase 'first chop' was used in the British Raj to mean 'highest quality'.

NOT MUCH CHOP

poor quality

93

'AVE A GO,
YA MUG!

*try harder,
you useless
individual!*

BARRACK FOR

support a sporting team or player

Originally, a Northern Irish word meaning 'to brag'.

HAPPY
AS LARRY
*extremely happy
or content*

H.G.'s
SPRAY

Not sure who the original
Larry was. Or how happy he was.
But from the photographic evidence
he was a riot in the right context.
Must've been great to have over for a
birthday or a family Christmas. The stories!
Sadly, Larry is no longer a contemporary
Australian first name. Dane and Bryce,
that's more like it. But 'happy as Dane'
and 'happy as Bryce' just don't
have the same authority.

BUNG

*not working;
injured*

Originally a
Yagara word,
from the
Brisbane area,
meaning 'dead'.

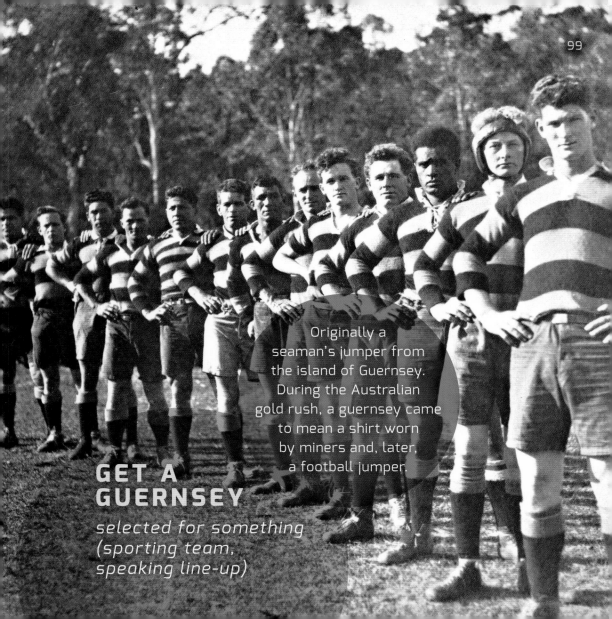

Originally a seaman's jumper from the island of Guernsey. During the Australian gold rush, a guernsey came to mean a shirt worn by miners and, later, a football jumper.

GET A GUERNSEY

selected for something (sporting team, speaking line-up)

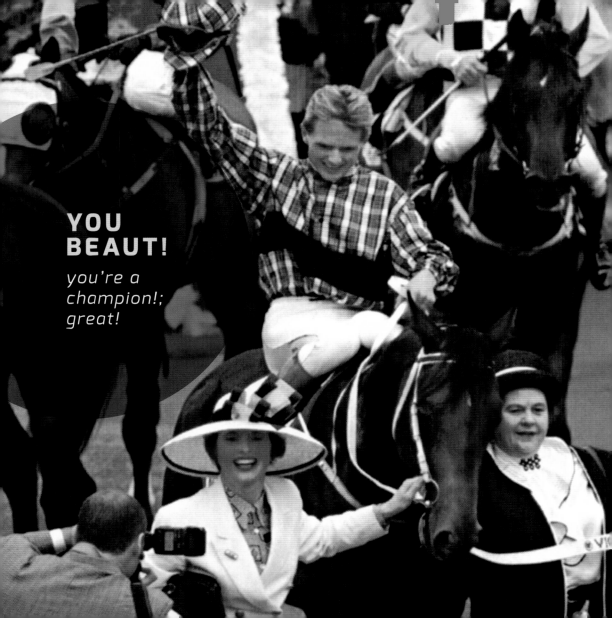

YOU BEAUT!

you're a champion!; great!

GIVE IT A BURL, SHIRL

give something a try

A *burl* is a 'spin' or 'whirl' in Scottish English. This phrase is a variation of the British, 'give it a whirl'.

FAIR CRACK OF THE WHIP!

you're not being fair!

FIT AS A MALLEE BULL

very strong and healthy

Mallee is probably an Aboriginal word from the area of western Victoria now known by that name.

EVERY MAN AND HIS DOG

everybody

CHOCKERS
full; overcrowded

Chock-a-block was a nautical phrase, probably used from the nineteenth century onwards, describing a block and tackle hoisted as high as possible.

LIST OF ILLUSTRATIONS

Many of these illustrations are details. For full images, see the National Library of Australia's catalogue at **nla.gov.au.**

cat-vn3995304, © Jeff Carter Archive; **48** Bruce Postle, *Farm Dog Bo Taking a Flying Leap up to a Hay Bale on the Back of a Truck*, 1991, nla.cat-vn4579127; **49** *A Happy New Year*, 1883, nla.cat-vn8078619; **50** Frank Hurley, *This Camera Caricature Shows Some Moulting Adélies Which Have Become Cluttered up with Snow during a Blizzard. The Three Birds to the Right Display Surprise at the Appearance of a Mate Which They Have Discovered Sheltering Behind a Hummock*, between 1911 and 1914, nla.cat-vn2384771; **51** *Alfred Marks and Jacki Weaver in the J.C. Williamson Production of Halfway up the Tree*, 1969, nla.cat-vn3068374; **52** Greg Barrett, *Steve Irwin Wrestling a Crocodile*, 2003, nla.cat-vn3806308; **54–55** Ern McQuillan, *Maternity Nurses Viewing X-rays at King George V Memorial Hospital, Sydney*, 1969, nla.cat-vn4984317; **56** *Wind Buffets the Bride's Veil and Train at the Wedding of Cyril Ritchard and Madge Elliott, St. Mary's Cathedral, Sydney*, 1935, nla.cat-vn3697874; **58** Rennie Ellis, *Mr Australia, Inflation*, 1980, nla.cat-vn4082239; **59** William Henry Corkhill, *Two Men Dressed in Running Clothes*, c.1900, nla.cat-vn558086; **60** Ern McQuillan, *A Man Modelling Day Wear*, 1966, nla.cat-vn4584810; **61** Axel Poignant, *Kangaroo, Sir Colin Mackenzie Zoological Park, Healesville, Victoria*, c.1947, nla.cat-vn4404452; **62–63** Rennie Ellis, *Yobbos, Sunbury Pop Festival*, 1974, nla.cat-vn4081901; **64** Don McMurdo, *Garry McDonald in Sugar Babies, Her Majesty's Theatre*, 1987, nla.cat-vn1606039; **65** Bob Nicol, *A Welcome Drink at the Mount Carbine Hotel for Cattlemen and Drivers of Cattle Transports*, 1971, nla.cat-vn4589902, Australian News and Information Bureau; **66–67** Rennie Ellis, *Robert DiPierdomenico 'Dipper', MCG*, 1986, nla.cat-vn4103266; **68** David Moore, *Outback Children, South Australia*, 1963, nla.cat-vn2258302; **69** *Tea under the Mulberry Tree*, page 29 in *The Australian Women's Weekly*, 7 January 1959, nla.news-page4912147; **70–71** Bill Bachman, *Noel Fullerton Riding Camel Malachi down a Sand Dune, Rainbow Valley, Northern Territory*, c.1982, nla.cat-vn5746467; **72** Jeff Carter, *Prawn Fisherman with Baskets of Prawns at Greenwell Point near Nowra, New South Wales*, c.1955, nla.cat-vn3991127, © Jeff Carter Archive; **74** *Impatiently Waiting for His Dinner*, 1939, nla.cat-vn3511892; **75** *Mr J. Harrington Talking with an Unidentified Man, New South Wales*, 1920s, nla.cat-vn6251139, courtesy Fairfax Syndication, www.fairfaxsyndication.com; **76** *Man Sitting on the Back of an Ostrich, Temora, New South Wales*, 1912, nla.cat-vn6334568, courtesy Fairfax Syndication, www.fairfaxsyndication.com; **77** Charles Troedel & Co., *Poor Dolly* (Melbourne: Australasian Sketcher, 1887), nla.cat-vn1844636; **79 (left)** John Tanner, *Surfers Paradise Sunbather*, 1963, nla.cat-vn4590501; **79 (right)** Isobel Bennett, *The Tiger Prawn Penaeus esclentus off Clarence River, Yamba, New South Wales*, 1986, nla.cat-vn4399767; **80** *Hot Work by Australian Gunners*, between 1939 and 1945, nla.cat-vn3578962; **81** R.W. Stuart, *Result of First Lesson*, 1862–1890s, nla.cat-vn3773747; **82** Bruce Howard, *Ned Kelly and a Medieval Lady at the Fancy Dress Ball at the Pub in Tennant Creek, Northern Territory*, 1972, nla.cat-vn4361475; **84** Rennie Ellis, *My Son Josh Learns to Swim*, 1972, nla.cat-vn4082332; **85** *Young Girl Holding a Large Apple beside Her Head, New South Wales*, 1930s, nla.cat-vn6342863, courtesy Fairfax Syndication, www.fairfaxsyndication.com; **86–87** Herbert H. Fishwick, *New Recruit Leaning out of a Train Window to Shake Hands with a Wounded Soldier, New South Wales*, c.1915, nla.cat-vn6329187, courtesy Fairfax Syndication, www.fairfaxsyndication.com; **88** Herbert H. Fishwick, *Study of a Bull Dog, New South Wales*, 1930s, nla.cat-vn6341783, courtesy Fairfax Syndication, www.fairfaxsyndication.com; **89** Michael Coyne, *Bachelor and Spinster Ball, Drinking from Boot, Finley, New South Wales*, 2006, nla.cat-vn3800775; **90** *Jack Hassen and Joe Brown during a Boxing Match at West Melbourne Stadium, Melbourne*, 1950, nla.cat-vn3646896; **92** Jeff Carter, *Tomorrow's Champion Wood Cutter, Berry, New South Wales*, 2003, nla.cat-vn4231273, © Jeff Carter Archive; **93** *Stephan Harold Gascoigne, Better Known as Yabba, King of the Unofficial Commentators on the Hill at the Sydney Cricket Ground*, c.1935, nla.cat-vn5126047; **94–95** Rennie Ellis, *SCG, The Hill, Sydney*, 1982, nla.cat-vn4088220; **96** *Smiling Man Wearing a Hat*, c.1900, nla.cat-vn4654413; **98** Rennie Ellis, *Rodney Marsh, MCG, Melbourne*, 1983, nla.cat-vn4085532; **99** *Nerang Football Team, Queensland*, 1930s, nla.cat-vn4558714; **100** Bruce Postle, *Trainer Gai Waterhouse Leads Nothin' Leica Dane and Jockey Shane Dye, after Winning the Victoria Derby at Flemington Racecourse, Melbourne*, 1995, nla.cat-vn4579493; **101** Bruce Howard, *Hal Connolly (USA), Who Won the Gold Medal in the Hammer Throw, Shows Boy Scout Julius Urban, 15, How the Spin Is Made at the Olympic Games Village at Heidelberg, Melbourne*, 1956, nla.cat-vn4306609; **102–103** Darren Clark, *Matthew Barrett Mustering on Avon Downs Cattle Station, Northern Territory*, 2013, nla.cat-vn6386881, courtesy Darren Clark; **104** *Portrait of Simon Spiteri Bending a Metal Bar Held in His Mouth*, c.1960, nla.cat-vn594779; **105** *Relatives Greeting Prisoners of War Arriving in Melbourne on the Oranje*, 1945, nla.cat-vn3107073; **106–107** Bob Peisley, *More Koalas for Lone Pine Sanctuary, Brisbane*, 1987, nla.cat-vn4082460, courtesy Australian Information Service; **114** *Five Beach Belles Wearing Tracksuits on Bondi Beach*, 1930, nla.cat-vn6291621, courtesy Fairfax Syndication, www.fairfaxsyndication.com

FAIR DINKUM!

ALPHABETICAL LIST OF TERMS

Mad as a gumtree full of galahs
crazy PAGE 48

Make a proper galah of yourself
make a fool of yourself PAGE 11

Miserable as a shag on a rock
very miserable PAGE 49

Mopey as a wet hen
dispirited; glum PAGE 48

No worries
that's okay; I don't mind PAGE 78

Not enough brains to give himself a headache
stupid PAGE 76

Not much chop
poor quality PAGE 92

Ocker
stereotypically unsophisticated
Australian PAGE 65

Off like a bucket of prawns in the sun
to leave quickly or soon PAGE 73

On the wallaby
on the move, looking for work PAGE 49

Panic merchant
a person who panics easily PAGE 64

Pash
a passionate kiss PAGE 31

Plonk
wine; cheap wine PAGE 45

Reg Grundies
underpants PAGE 59

Rough as guts
coarse; uncouth PAGE 89

Running around like a chook with its head cut off
panicking; overreacting PAGE 69

Sanger
sandwich PAGE 36

See you round like a rissole
goodbye; see you later PAGE 19

She'll be right
things will be okay PAGE 84

She's apples
everything's fine PAGE 85

Silly duffer
a person who has made a silly mistake
PAGE 65

Snag
sausage PAGE 37

Stone the crows!
wow!; I can't believe it!; I'm unimpressed
PAGE 51

Strewth!
that's shocking!; wow!; that was close!
PAGE 53

Suss
suspicious; suspect PAGE 35

Things are crook in Tallarook
things are not going well PAGE 78

True blue
authentically Australian PAGE 33